AF507003

A Book of Books
A Book of Lists
A List of Books
Book of Titles
A Titles of Books
A Book of Authors
A List of Author Books
A Book of Lists of Titles and Author Book

A Book

by
ANDREW A. FELDER

Total Word Count 5,416

Font: Chalkboard Book Dimensions 5" x 8"
Total # of pages: (See last page and add 4.)

<u>Frequency of Appearance of Selected Words</u>

Dinner – 4

Pain – 4

Promise – 1

Subconscious – 0

Whisper – 0

Cat – 3

Down – 14

Out – a lot

Crap – 0

Relevance – 0

"I could have written many of these books myself and maybe I still will. Apparently, no one has yet." Neva Putoff (*'Til Tomorrow*)

"To be, or not to be? That's a question. Whether 'tis nobler in the mind to read or not to read this book while my unheeded garden grows to seed…. that's a question for Tamara. Maybe Alaska." Saul Lillow-Kwee (*Books as Doorstops*)

"This book is…like…addictive!" Hera Wynn

HUMOR FICTION HISTORY PHILOSOPHY NON-FICTION BIOGRAPHY SELF HELP COOKING

SCIENCE TRAVEL MYSTERY HEALTH CHILDREN'S BUSINESS HOME & GARDEN SATIRE

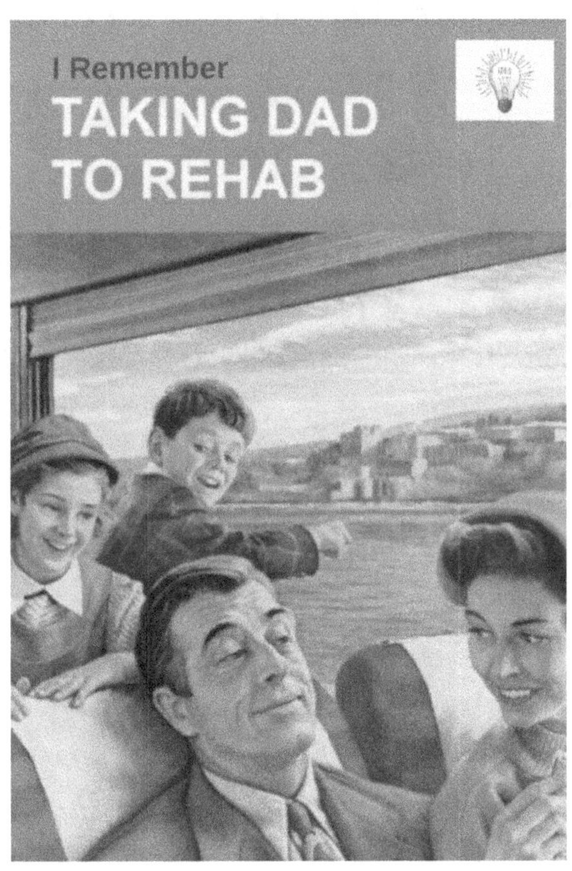

I Remember
TAKING DAD
TO REHAB

Ambulance Driver
by Adam Mehway

Broke
by M.T. Wallet

Caste Away
by Gupta Amin Patel

Down For The Count
by Sara Tonin

It's All In The Game
by Manny Attier Astufal

Causing Pain
by Otis Leghurts

Crackdown
by Lauren Order

Wasting Away
by Fester N. Lagoons

The Great Flood
by Noah Zark

Fading Away
by Peter Innout

Sherlock Holmes Does it Again
by Scott Linyard

I Like it Rough
by Mona Lott

I Never Promised You
by A. Rose Garten

Neither a Borrower
by Nora Lender Bee

The German Bank Robbery
by Hans Zupp

Never Signal Defeat
by Flip DeByrd

On The Hot Seat
by Erasmus B. Burnon

Palace in the Desert
by Cammie Lott

Peeping Tom
by Sawyer Panties

Playing with the Christmas Fire
by Yul B. Sari

Pub Crawl
by Carrie Meholm

Stop Shouting
by Danielle Soloud

Without Warning
by Oliver Sudden

Slipped Disk
by Lord Howard Hertz

Keep Falling On Your Head
by Rayn Dropz

Kissing Makes It Better
by Bessa Mae Mucho

Night Blindness
by Cansey Forchette

Looking For Mr. Right
by Anita Blackman and Ray
Smatters

Split Personalities
by Jacqueline Hyde

Superhero in Gotham
by U. De Mann

Suspense
by Cliff Hanger

The Big Wave
by Sue Nahmi

SATIRE

HOME & GARDEN

BUSINESS

CHILDREN'S

HEALTH

MYSTERY

TRAVEL

SCIENCE

The Fall Of A Watermelon
by S. Platt

The Bullfighter
by Matt Adore

The Island Chain
by Archie Pellago

The Glass Bikini
by Seymour Skynn

Fastest Gun in the West
by Everett DeReddy

The Monkey's Cage
by Jim Panzee

Breaking the Law
by Kermit A. Kryme

The Trial Lawyer
by Tess Temoni

The Hitchhiker
by Juana Lift

A Tight Situation
by Leah Tard

The Last Prayer
by Ben E. Dixon

Lost Cause
by Noah Vale

The Last Prayer
by Ben E. Dixon

The Lion Tamer
by Claudia Bottom

The Long Walk Home
by Misty Buss

The Nude Beach
by Seymour Hair

The Scent of a Man
by Jim Nasium

The Smell in the Vatican
by Pope Porree

The Squeaky Gate
by Rusty Hinges

The Cloakroom Attendant
by Mahatma Coats

Tigger's Revenge
by Claude Balls

Tight Situation
by Leah Tard

Too Rough
by Soren Redd

No!
by Kurt Reply

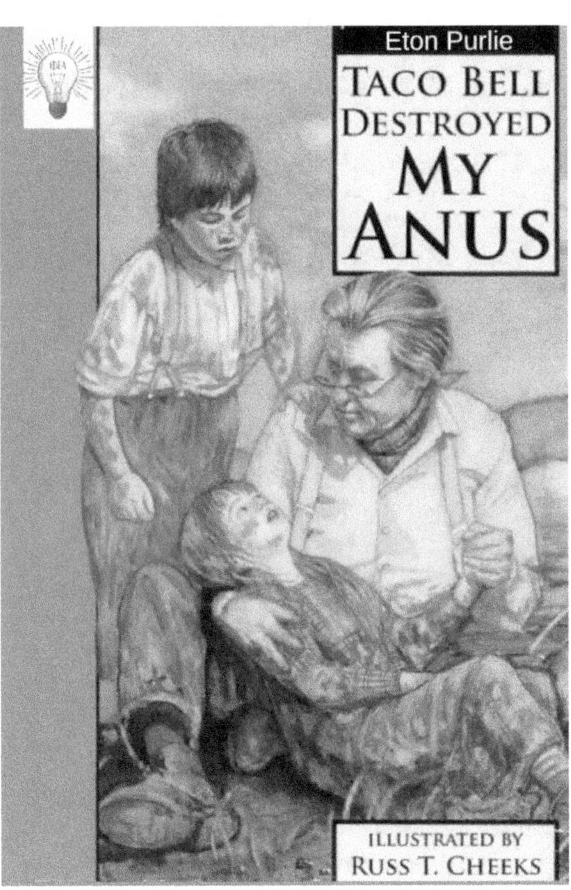
Eton Purlie
TACO BELL DESTROYED MY ANUS
ILLUSTRATED BY
RUSS T. CHEEKS

Mexican Revenge
by Monty Zuma

Trails in the Sand
by Dick Dragon

If Tomorrow Never Comes
by Stu Laite

Unsolved Mysteries
by N. Igma

Too Rough
by Soren Redd

A Matter of Chemistry
by Farrah Mone

Answering the Questions of the
Universe
by Howard I. Know

Without Warning
by Oliver Sutton

Assault With Battery
by Eva Ready

Wouldn't You Know It?
by Murphy Slaw

A Spy in the King's Court
by Sir Valence Camera

I'll Never Stop Loving You
by Percy Vere

Shakespeare in the Desert
by Cam L. Ott

Yoko's Robe
by Kim Ono

Good Works
by Ben Evolent

Sail Around the World
by Madge Ellen

HUMOR · FICTION · HISTORY · PHILOSOPHY · NON-FICTION · BIOGRAPHY · SELF HELP · COOKING

The Cat's Revenge

by Claude Bottom

Without Value

by Hugh Sless

Blowout!

by Vlad Tyre

Jaws

by Tay Kabyte

Out of Breath

by Ima Puffing

Keep Out!

by Barb Dwyer

Desert Crossing

by I. Rhoda Camel

The Teenage Werewolf

by Harry Boddy

Great Mysteries
by Hugh Dunnit

Free Willy
by Freda Wale

Downpour
by Wayne Dwops

Dive! Dive!
by Perry Scope

Broken Window
by Eva Brick

Land Ahoy
by I.C. Fields

Without Warning
by Oliver Sudden

Animal Scents
by Farrah Mones

Cheating on His Wife
by Izzy Bakyet

In Farmer MacGregor's Garden
by Peter Abbott

One Hundred Years Old
by Abbie Birthday

Indiana Jones' Adventures
by Darren Rescue

Gone With The Wind
by George Uh

Gangway!
by Hedda Steam

Pressure Relief
by My Korsetsov

Mystery in the Barnyard
by Hu Flung Dung

The Meat Eaters
by Carney Vore

Crackdown!
by Lauren Order

The Candy Store
by Pepper Mintz

Shellfire
by R. Tillery

The Bishop's Seat
by Cathy Drall

Plunging Neckline
by Seymour Bust

Waiting for Dinner
by Sally Vating

Dull Razor
by Nick Shaving

Breaking In

by Jimmy DeLock

Outdoor Cooking

by Barbie Cue

Music of the Early 1960s

by Tristan Shout

Arriba

by Juan Tanamerra

Computer Memories

by Meg Abight

Pressure Relief

by My Korsetzov

Events in The Former Soviet Union

by Perry Stroyka

The Good Breakfast

by Hammond Deggs

Where to Put Your Money
by Bill Fold

Mountain Climbing
by Andover Hand

Acrophobia Explained
by Alfredo Heights

American Breakfast
by Chris P. Bacon

Pancakes
by Mabel Sirrup

Bricklaying
by Bill Jerome Wall

Exotic Irish Plants
by Phil O'Dendron

Animal Ailments
by Ann Thrax

Using Credit Cards to Your Advantage
by Bill Melater

Head Of Security
by Barb Dwyer

Vegas Divorces
by Marion Hayste

Transportation in the Middle Ages
by Orson Cart

Acronyms
by Anna Graham

French Cars
by Myra Neault

How to Break In To Anything
by Jimmy DeLock

Many Are Cold, But Few Are
Frozen
by Minnie Sota

The LA Lakers' Breakfast
by Kareem O'Wheat

Updating the Tax Codes
by Lou Polls

Financial Insecurity
by Wilma Monilast

Sea Birds
by Al Batross

Presidential Press Briefs
by Colonel O'Truth and Lotta Lies

Why You Need Insurance
by Justin Case

Everything About Vegetables
by Brock Lee

Geology

by Roxanne Minerals

The Department of Redundancy Department (Backing Up the Bureaucracy)

by Phil Phillips, Tom Thomas and Robert Roberts

A Bestiary of Plant Eaters

by Herb Avore

Animal Scents

by Farrah Mones

Things To Do At Parties

by Bob Frapples

The Philippine Post Office

by Imelda Letta

The Russian Mafia

by Ewil Kuturnutzof

A Year Without St Patrick's Day
by Erin Gogh-Braughless

Armed Heists
by Robin Banks

Stand-up Comedian
by Joe Kerr

Vegas Divorces
by Marion Hayste

A Boxing Cornerman's Story
by Dawson DeTowel

Lazy Employees
by Hans Doolittle

It's Magic!
by Sven Galli

Was OJ Guilty?
by Howard I. Noh

HUMOR

FICTION

HISTORY

PHILOSOPHY

NON-FICTION

BIOGRAPHY

SELF HELP

COOKING

The Over-Population of Paris
by Francis Crowded

Interior Decorating
by Curt Enrod

Russian Dry Cleaning
by U. Dropov and U. Pikkup

The Truancy Problem
by Marcus Absent

More of a Lute Than a Guitar
by Amanda Lynne

The Traveling Pants Sisterhood
by Hugh Jassis

1776
by Bertha Fanashun

Revealing The Magician's Secrets
by Howie Dudat

The Caste System in America

by Aymsa Pritty

Private Parts

by Jenny Talia

A Little Bit of Everything

by Samora Dissendat

How to Draw

by Ellis Strait

It's All In Your Head

by Madge Enation

Days of the Revolution

by Millie Tant

The Scent of a Man

by Jim Nasium

Disappeared!

by Otto Sight

The Lion Attack
by Claude Miarmoff

The Monkey's Cage
by Jim Panzee

My Apologies
by Hamza Sari

Puppet on a String
by Marie Annette Maker

The History of Exxon
by Phil Errup

Desert Storm
by Dustin Minose

Eating Disorders
by Anna Rexia

The Story Behind Smokey the
Bear Rangers
by Forrest Feyar

The Songs Of "South Pacific"
by Sam and Janet Evening

A Man of Habit
by Rich Ewell

Stars and Stripes
by Jose Canusey

A Great Plenty
by E. Nuff

The Industrial Revolution
by Otto Mattick

Artificial Weightlessness
by Andy Gravity

Color Blind
by Rachel Animus

Allegiance to the King
by Neil Downe

#1 NATIONAL BESTSELLER
TILLERSON
The Art of Dealing with a Moron
REX W. TILLERSON with DONALD TRUMP

More or Less
by Marge Inoverra

Sleep Apnea
by Constance Snoring

The Star Wars Diet
by Obese Juan Kenobi

Urintology
by Ima Pither
(translated from Sanskit by
Major Tinkle)

Soap Opera Guide
by Dee Young & Dee Restless

Unemployed
by Anita Job

Interior Decorating
by Curt Enrod

SATIRE

HOME & GARDEN

BUSINESS

CHILDREN'S

HEALTH

MYSTERY

TRAVEL

SCIENCE

Chinese Toy Recalls
by Sam Ting Wong

Chinese Apathy
by Hu Cares

Geez, It's Hot!
by Mike Hammeldyed

My Seventh Husband
by Ivana Newhouse

Split Personalities
by Jacqueline Hyde

Feeding the World
by Diana Hunger

Bad Gardeners
by Wilt Ed Plants

Aging Without Grace
by Ova Dahill

Grave Mistakes
by Paul Bearer

The Last of Twelve
by Dee Sember

Kindergarten Kop
by Bea Hayve

Modern Giants
by Hugh Mungous

Making Explosives
by Stan Wellback

The First of Twelve
by Jan Yuary

Fat Lady in The Sideshow
by Ellie Funt

House Construction
by Bill Jerome Holme

Kangaroo Illnesses
by Marcus Walla by, M.D.

Exotic Irish Plants
by Phil O'Dendron

Musical Gunfighters
by The Okay Chorale

A Whole Lot of Cats
by Kitt N. Caboodle

I Work with Diamonds
by Jules Sparkle

Lawyers and Suffering
by Grin and Barrett

Flogging in the Army
by Corporal Punishment

Errors and Accidents
by Miss Takes and Miss Haps

Where to Find Islands
by Archie Pelago

French Overpopulation
by Francis Crowded

Monkey Shines
by Bob Boone

Why Cars Stop
by M.T. Tank

Turtle Racing
by Hubie Quick

Military Rule
by Marshall Law

I Like Liquor
by Ethyl Alcohol

I Love Crowds
by Morris Merrier

The Yellow River

by I. P. Freely

Off To Market

by Tobias A. Pigg

A Great Plenty

by E. Nuff

Mosquito Bites

by Ivan Itch

My Lost Causes

by Noah Vale

Grave Mistakes

by Paul Bearer

Get Out There!

by Sally Forth

Red Vegetables

by B. Troot

Highway Travel
by Dusty Rhodes

It's a Shocker
by Alec Tricity

I Hit the Wall
by Isadore There

Swimming in the Arctic
by I. C. Waters

Laughing in the White House
by Polly Tickle

I Love Mathematics
by Adam Up

He's Contagious!
by Lucas Measles

Hide and Seek
by I.C. Yu

Cooking
With
Pooh
Yummy Tummy
Cookie Cutter
Treats

Banquet at McDonalds
by Tommy Ayk

Green Lawn Chairs
by Patty O'Furniture

Jewelry Collecting
by Pearl Nicholas

I'm an Atheist
by Noel Noevon

My Long Walk
by Misty Bus

The Hitchhiker
by Juan Nalift

Weepy Movie
by Maud Lynn Storey

We're All Flakes
by Dan Druff

May Flowers
by April Showers

It's Unfair!
by Wi Me

Breaking the Law
by Kermit A. Krime

In the Arctic Ocean
by Isa Berg

Your Future
by Claire Voyant

Ready, Set ….
by Sadie Werd

Jagged Fingernails
by I. Bittem

Pull with All You've Got
by Eve Ho

A Ham Radio Primer
by Loudon Clear

Daddy, Are We There Yet?
by Miles Away

Equine Leg Cramps
by Charlie Horse

The Miracle Drug
by Penny Sillin

Hypnotism
by N. Tranced

Party On, Dude
by Jill Out & Ray Zinhel

The Bird Collection
by Arnie Thologee

The Economy is Recovering!
by Knott Kwite

The Effects of Alcohol
by Sir Osis of DeLiver

Tug of War
by Paul Hard

You Wash, I'll Dry
by Terry Cloth

The Lumberjack
by Tim Burr

Candle-Vaulting
by Jack B. Nimble

Surprised!
by Omar Gosh

Genie in a Bottle
by Grant Wishes

Feelings
by Cara Lott

All Alone
by Saul E. Terry

The Car Capital of The World
by Mitch Egan

Rich People
by Bill Yeneer

Six Drinks Too Many
by Taiwan Ahn

Rusty Bed Springs
by I.P. Nightly

Mobile Homes
by Winnie Bago

Fixing Computer Programs
by Dee Bugger

Handel's Messiah
by Ollie Looya

Battle Axes
by Tom A. Hawk

Big Fart!
by Hugh Jass

Children's Songbook
by Skip Tumalu

Drafted!
by Abel Bodeed

Ex-Presidential Retreat
by Kenny Bunkport

Ithaca Colleges
by Cora Nell

Clothes for Germ Kings
by Mike Robes

Judo and Jujitsu
by Marsha Lartz

Banquet at McDonalds
by Tommy Ake

Hunger in America
by Heywood Jafeedme

I'm Someone Else
by Ima Nonna-Muss

Lawyers of Suffering
by Grinn and Barrett

Stunned Over Christmas
by Holly Daze

Advantageous
by Benny Fishall

The Music Of Sammy Davis Jr.
by Candy Mann

We Take Credit Cards, But...
by Cassius Best

Under the Bleachers
by Seymour Butts

Counting to Ten
by Wuan Too

Bacteria
by Mike Robes

Beguiled
by N. Tysing

The Empty Glass
by Phil D. Cupp

Am I Bothered?
by Carrie-Ann N.E. Way

Amphibians
by Newt and Sally Mander

Contempt for Human Nature
by Miss Ann Thropy

Drinking to Excess
by Al Koholic

Good bye Cruel World
by Sue A. Seid

Implants
by E. Norma Stitz

Try Harder
by Buster Gutt

Underwear Problems
by Lucy Lastic

Seaside Amusements
by Penny R. Cade

Still Looking for My Heart
by Sam Francisco

How to Find a Husband
by Amanda Kiss

SATIRE
HOME & GARDEN
BUSINESS
CHILDREN'S
HEALTH
MYSTERY
TRAVEL
SCIENCE

True Love is Within Your Grasp
by Jack Imhoff

The Art of French Kissing
by Sam Paypa Tong

New Mexico Tour Book
by Albie Kierky

What to Look for in a Hotel
by Mary Ott

A Guide to Desert Highways
by Dusty Rhodes

Swimming in the Arctic
by I. C. Waters

Baseball's Greatest Hits
by Homer

A Hole in The Bucket
by Lee King

Chicago Gangs of the 30s
by Tommy Gunn

How To Prevent Leaks
by Titus A. Drum

Not Bogged Down by Reality
by Jason Rainbows

Exploring Other Galaxies
by Anne Dromeda

The Shrinking Society
by Les Ismor

The Fortuneteller
by Reid Palms and Crystal Ball

Erotic Adventures
by Oliver Klozoff

Strong Winds
by Gayle Force

HOME & GARDEN SATIRE

BUSINESS

CHILDREN'S

HEALTH

MYSTERY

SCIENCE TRAVEL

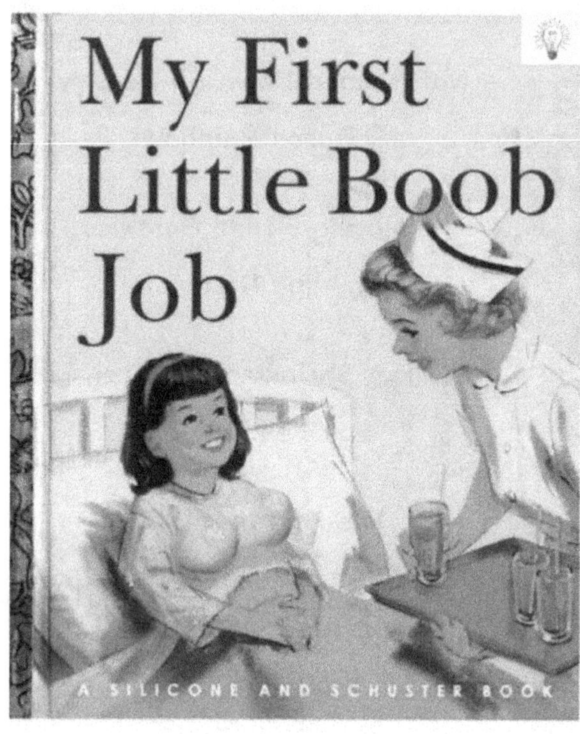

Ladies' Man
by Phil Anderer

The Industrial Revolution
by Otto Mattick

Danger!
by Luke Out

Astronauts in Space
by Landon Moon

Don't Let the Son Go Down on Me
by Jonna Elton

Elvis Impersonator
by Amal Shukkup

My Youth in Detroit
by Helen Earth

Leo Tolstoy
by Warren Peese

Lewis Carroll

by Allison Wonderland

My Life as a Fortune Teller

by I. Reid Palms

The Irish Heart Surgeon

by Angie O'Plasty

The French Chef - A Biography

by Sue Flay

I Was the Wizard of Oz

by Ima Munchkin

Yassir

by Yirma 'Bebe' Nau

The Light of the Day

by Gladys Knight

My Life of Crime

by Robin Banks

NASCAR Speedsters
by Red E. Setgo

Crazy From Birth
by Lou Screws

Gunslingers With Gas
by Wyatt Burp

Wo Is Me
by Allen Wo

Still in the Closet
by Ward Robe

Ghandan With the Wind
by Kofi Kaykfahtz

Growing Up Castrating
by Ivana Kutyurnutzov

The Man Who Shot
by LeeBert T. Valence

Crocodile Dundee

by Ali Gator

Binge Drinking Spots in Taipei

by Taiwan Ahn

The Announcer's Handbook

by Mike Rafone

My Life With Annette

by Amos Kateer

The Chuck Berry Story

by Judy Frudy

The Lady Pirate

by Peg Legg

Whatever It Is, I Didn't Do It!

by Ivan Alibi

Personal Best

by Marco D. Stinkshin

Making A Difference
by Sam Ting

Because I Said So
by Frank O. Pinyan

With The Stars
by Dan Sing

My Career As A Clown
by Abe Ozo

My Rules For Living
by Sharon Sharalike

Not Bogged Down in Reality
by Jason A. Rainbow

Me and My Big Mouth
by Monica Lewinsky

Oh Snap!
by Joe Mamma

Robots

by Anne Droid

It's Magic!

by Sven Gali

April Fools

by Sue Prize

Come On In

by Doris Open

Parachuting Over the Cliff

by Hugo First

Many Are Cold, But Few Are

Frozen

by Minnie Sota

Life Before Cars

by Orson Buggy

Fun at the Circus

by Taymond DeLyons

Songs For Children
by Barbra Blacksheep

Silly Rabbit
by Trixie R. Forkids

Say The Magic Word
by Abby Cadabra

Rapunzel, Rapunzel
by Harris Long

Joe Wins at the Track Meet
by C. Howie Runns

Don't Be Scared
by Emma Fraid

Cry Wolf
by Al Armist

A Stuntman to The End
by Kenny Duitt

A Trip to the Dentist
by Yin Pain & Lord Howard Hertz

Horrendous!
by Terry Bull

Los Angeles Pachyderms
by L.A. Funt

Life in Chicago
by Wendy City

Wind In the Maple Trees
by Russell Ingleaves

The Bog
by Pete Maas

String Instruments
by Viola Player

Prepare To Meet Your Maker
by Eva DeStruckshun

Mosquito Bites
by Ivan Itch

Just Say No
by Will Power

As Solid As....
by Rocco Gibraltar

Athletic Supporter
by Jacques Strap

What We Want
by Moe and Lotta Money

40 Yards to the Outhouse
by Willy Makit and Betty Wont

The NHL Today
by Stanley Kupp

Pitching to the Corners
by Justin Seid

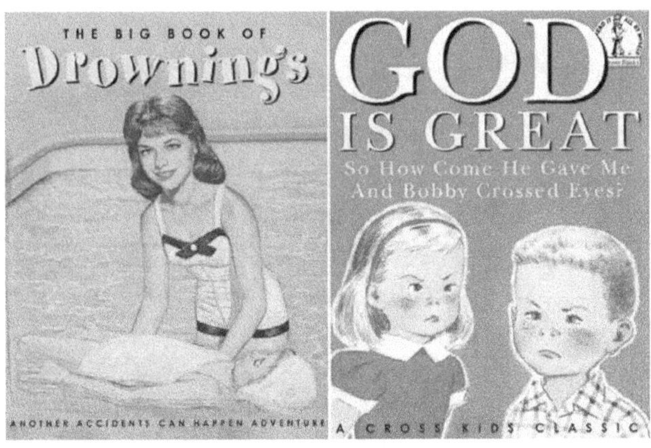

HUMOR
FICTION
HISTORY
PHILOSOPHY
NON-FICTION
BIOGRAPHY
SELF HELP
COOKING

SATIRE
HOME & GARDEN
BUSINESS
CHILDREN'S
HEALTH
MYSTERY
TRAVEL
SCIENCE

The Greatest Tennis Matches

by Davis Skupp

Full Moon

by Seymour Bunz

Mystery in the Barnyard

by Hu Flung Dung

Screwed to the Wall

by Molly Bolt

Archery

by Beau N. Arrow

Party On!

by Barnaby Wild

Artificial Clothing

by Polly Ester

Sore Joints

by A. King

My Life of Crime
by Robin Banks

Completely Out of It
by Stu Poor

Anything But Clear
by Andy Guity

Exercise on Wheels
by Cy Kling

Gardening With The Ex-President
by Rose Bush

Hertz, Don't It?
by Lisa Carr

Small Treasures in the Toilet
Bowl
by I.P. Nickels

Southern California Waffles
by Sandy Eggo

Punk Rock Rules!
by Lotta Noyze

The Peace Mission
by Olive Branch

What's Your Invention?
by Pat Tent

Boy Scout's Handbook
by Casey Needzit

Brane Surjery Maid Simpel
by Sarah Bellum

Body Parts
by Anne Attomi

Confessions Of A Gold Digger
by Emile Ticket

Guarding the Door
by Sergeant Attarms

Bubbles in the Bathtub

by Iva Windybottom

Noise is Forbidden!

by Nada Loud

Foods to Avoid

by O. Beets

Not Too Hot, Not Too Cold

by Luke Quarm

Outer Space

by A. Leanne

The National Science Foundation

by Grant Money

Some Like it Sweet

by Sugar Cane

Some Like it Hot

by Red Pepper

How to Succeed in School
by Rita Book

Outgoing Personality
by Greg Arius

I Wuz Framed!
by Gil Tee

My Life As A Comic
by Stan Dupp

Skunks in the Shrubbery
by P. Yew

The TV News Anchorman
by Maury Ports

The History of Fox TV
by Annette Work

I Wish I'd Never Been Born
by Rudy Day

Digital

by Anna Logg

Outstanding

by Emma Nentley

Over and Out

by Roger Wilko

Diplomatic Mission

by M. Bassy

Office Software

by Mike Rowsoft

An Optician's Guide

by Seymour Clearly

Dinner Delight

by Roland Butter

Recommended Books

by Betty Dreedit

Empathy
by Ophelia Sadness

Relay Race
by Anne Dover-Baton

Foot Coverings
by Susan Socks

Crossing the Atlantic in a
Rowboat
by Willy Makit

Rubber Inflatables
by Abel Loon

Rusty Bedsprings
by I. P. Knightly

Hair Today, Gone Tomorrow
by I. M. Balding

Magnificent
by Wanda Full

Triumphant Conquest
by Vic Tree

Classic Groceries
by Chopin Liszt

Clear Sky Forecast
by Esau Starrs

Do You Hear a Phone?
by Isabel Ringen

Rushing
by Ed Long

Different Ways to Spell 'Bob'
by Robert Roberts

Errors and Accidents
by Ms. Takes and Ms. Haps

Mardi Gras Time
by Lou Esiana

Neat Shirts
by Preston Ironed

Maritime Disasters
by Andrea Doria

Tighten That Butt!
by A. Nall Retentif

Meeting in France
by Ron DeVous

Going Nuts!
by Cy Cosis

New Mexico Tour Book
by Albie Kerky

Pentagon Press Releases
by Colonel O'Truth and Lotta Lies

Little Bitty Froggies
by Tad Pole

Tear Up Those Betting Slips
by Lou Zerr

The Bog
by Pete Maas

Uninteresting Road Signs
by Bill Bored

Walking Tall
by G. Raffe

TV—Not!
by Ray Deough

How I Won the Marathon
by Randy Hallway

The Non-Believer
by Hera Tick

Hark The Herald
by Harold B. Thighname

THE
BEGINNER'S GUIDE
TO
SEX IN THE
AFTERLIFE
An Exploration
of the
Extraordinary
Potential of
Sexual Energy

What's the
Difference?
by Alda Saim Toomey

Never Put
Off 'til
Tomorrow…
(what you can put off
indefinitely)
My path from being an amateur
crastinator to turning 'pro'.
by Candace Waite

The Secret Hideaway
by P. Ed DaTerre

Held Hostage by Terrorists
by Aldo Anything

Here's Puss in Your Eye
by Lance Boyle

I'm Nothing Without You
by M. T. Ness

The Speedster Wins the Race
by C. Howie Runns

Loudspeakers
by Mike Rofone

Never Forget
by L. E. Funt

Perverted Tales
by M. Morel

Real-Life Lottery Winners
by Jack Potts

Preparing Leather
by Tanya Hyde

Shakespearian Phrases
by Toby R. Nottoby

Part Of Her
by Oliver Knott

Something's Out There
by Will B. Watchenu

Reach For the Stars
by Tippy Toes

No More Circuit Breakers!
by Ira Fuse

I Won the Lottery
by Candice B. Trew

Keep 'Em That Way
by Private Parts

Old Furniture Refinished
by Ann Teak

On The Road to Recovery
by Will Being

Talking Gossip
by Phyllis Zinn

The Unknown Rodent
by A. Noni Maus

Whatchamacallit!
by Thingum A. Bobb

Racketeering
by Dennis Court

How to Really Annoy Anyone
by Aunt Agonize

A Tourist's Guide to Mali
by Tim Buck II

Cheaper than IBM
by P.C. Clone

College Athletics
by N.C. Dubblelay

The Employee Handbook
by Ernie Living

Don't Tread On Me
by Amanda B. Reckonwith

Home of the Liberty Bell
by Phil A. Delphia

I Can Fix It
by Jerry Rigg

Boring Midwestern Cities
by Cole Lumbus

Columbus, Magellan and & the
Great Explorers
by Enzo DiUrth

Turkey Parts
by Eton Drumsticks

Knock, Knock
by Annie Buddihome

Girl On a Budget
by Penny Pincher

Broken Window
by Eva Brick

The Chinese Arsonist
by Kin Dling

If I Invited Him....
by Woody Kum

The Gem State
by Ida Hoe

Spotted Pooch
by: Dale Mation

Crime & Punishment in the USA
by Penny Tenshury

Modern Dentistry
by Phil McCavitee

Frogs and Newts
by Anne Fibienz

The Capacity to Endure
by Sue Stainability

Antlers in the Tree Top
by Hu Goosta Mouse

Brown Spots on the Wall
by Hu Flung Pooh

Do I Look Fat?
by Donna Gogh-Dere

Don't Come Back Again
by Doris Shutt

Stone Age
by Neil Ithic

Misunderstood
by Art Tystic

The Prayer Circle
by Hans Joyned

Fred Can Philosophize
by Immanuel Kant

Hanging Around
by Stacy Moore

The Wring Turn
by Misty Eggzit

Cooking With Noodles
by Ravi Oley

Safari Concerns
by Lionel Eecha

The Life of a Dog
by Kaye Nein

Okee Dokee
by Roger Wilco

The Business of Raising Flowers
by Flo Wrist

A Smoker's Addiction
by Nick O'Teen

The First Book of Snakes
by Anna Conda

Prison Escape
by Jay L. Byrd

Baffled!
by Ken Fusion

The Beat of My Heart
by Steffi Scope

Computer Memories
by Meg Abight

The Task Ahead
by Howell I. Evert Dudiss

Massachusetts Vacation Spots
by Nan Tuckett

The Mythical Horse
by U. Nick Horne

Why Use Credit Cards?
by Bill Melater

It Was Meant to Be
by Destiny Nau

Measles
by Rash Oliver

Raise Your Arms

by Harry Pitts

Believe Me!

by Ima Lyre

The Great Escape

by Freida Convict

The Smell in the Vatican

by Pope Porrie

You're My Everything

by Trudy Light

Walking In the Moonlight

by Holden Hanz

Nuclear Explosives

by Adam Baum

Razing Buildings

by Dina Mite

When I grow up
I want to be
Pretentious
3b
Key Words
Reading Scheme

TWO FULL-LENGTH JAKE HUNTER NOVELS!
WHO ATE
THE DAMN
PIZZA ROLLS
15¢
I SWEAR TO GOD,
I AM GOING TO SHOOT YOU
IN YOUR STUPID FACE
IF YOU ATE THEM ALL
ALSO: THE CASE OF THE
GIRL WHO WAS SHOT
IN HER STUPID FACE

HUMOR FICTION HISTORY PHILOSOPHY NON-FICTION BIOGRAPHY SELF HELP COOKING

Hope for the Blind
by Wanda Seymore

Adding Fractions
by Lois D. Nominator

I've Told You Many Times Before
by Ferdi Lastime

The Coroner's Assistant
by I. Doug Graves

Imitating Mozart
by Sam Phony

'Pampered and Indulged
by Molly Coddled

Falling Off a Bridge
by Ilene Dover

Spilling My Guts
by N. Trayles

The Nail Files
by Emma-Ree Board

And Shut Up!
by Sid Downe

Senior Board Games
by Bing O. Iwin

The Mandarin Gold Rush
by Quan Dyke

Scat, Go Away!
by Ron Onhome

How to Get An "A" On Your Math
Exam
by Cal Q. Lator

Goes
by Ann E. Ting

How Things Work
by Reid D. Manuel

Fluffy Pillows
by Heather Downe

Ecclesiastical Infractions
by Cardinal Sin

Biblical Conception
by Emma Q. Layte

How to Cut Grass
by Lon Moore

Timepieces With Faces
by Anna Logg

Oh, What A Relief It Is
by Al Cassell-Zerr

Swimming in the Arctic
by I. C. Waters

The Great Flood
by Noah Zark

You Don't Say
by Ida Claire

Greenhouse Flowers
by Mary Golds

What She Gave Me
by Irv Erginitee

Singing Without Music
by Al Capella

50 Ways to Leave Your Lover
by Howie "Gunner" Dudiss

Overcoming Nervousness on Radio
by Mike Fright

Positive Reinforcement
by Wade Duhgo

How to Read a Book
by Paige Turner

312 Ways to Die
by Sue I. Syed

After The Corned Beef And
Cabbage
by Kay O'Pectate

Feeling Blue
by Perry Winkle

The Campaign of 1964
by Bayh and Lodge

Pain Relief
by Ann L. Gesick

The Proctologist's Handbook
by Ben Dover

Look 10 Years Younger
by Fay Slift

Plumbing for Dummies
by Dwayne D. Pipe

Positive Reinforcement
by Wade Agoh

Idiot's Guide to Bullfighting
by Matt Adore

Tighten That Butt!
by A. Nayle Retentive

Winning the Race
by Vic Tree

Growing Old Gracefully
by Jerry Attrick

Making Explosives
by Stan Wellback

Why it Won't Work
by Mel Function

Good Housekeeping
by Lottie Dust

SATIRE · HOME & GARDEN · BUSINESS · CHILDREN'S · HEALTH · MYSTERY · TRAVEL · SCIENCE

Stop Arguing
by Xavier Breath

Scandinavian Photography
by Matt Finnish

Soak Your Ex-Husband
by Ali Money

Nordic Groundskeeping Secrets
by Leif Raker

Don't Do Anything Rash
by Jacques Itch

Bathroom Etiquette
by Ivana Tinkle

Caulking Made Easy
by Phil DeKrevis

Move Your Body
by Sheikh Aleg

Car Repairs
by Axel Grease

Do Your Own Housework
by Dustin Cook

DoIt Yourself
by Tyrone Shoelaces

French Windows
by Pattie O'Dors

Crosswords and Word Search
by E. Nigma

I Don't Know What
by Jenna. Sekwah

Preparing Your Last Will and
Testament
by Benny Fishery

It' A Wonderful Day!
by Fay-Lynn Gruvie

SATIRE

HOME & GARDEN

BUSINESS

CHILDREN'S

HEALTH

MYSTERY

TRAVEL

SCIENCE

Making New Friends
by Wah Tsieu Naim

Empathy
by Ophelia Sadness

A Boxing Cornerman's Story
by Dawson DeTowel

Fat Lady In The Sideshow
by Ellie Funt

The French Chef
by Sue Flay

Bad Gardener
by Will Ted Plant

Take a Break!
by Colin Sick

How to Make Your Wife Happy
by Dick C. Normos

A Guide to Binge Drinking
by Carrie Meholm

Guide To Mixology
by Bart Ender

Cooking Spaghetti
by Al Dente

Looking for God
by Zeke Enyulfind

Neither A Borrower
by Nora Lender-Bee

Overcoming Acrophobia
by Alfredo Hytes

The Perils of Drug Addiction
by Anita Fixx

Breakfast – The Most Important
Meal of the Day
by Hammond Deggs

SATIRE

HOME & GARDEN

BUSINESS

CHILDREN'S

HEALTH

MYSTERY

TRAVEL

SCIENCE

Take This Job and Shove It!
by Ike Witt

Do it Now!
by Igor Beaver

50 years in the Saddle
by Major Asburn

Back Row of the Orchestra
by Clara Nett

Mensa Man
by Gene Yuss

A Teenager in the 50s
by Bobbie Sox

Inflammation, Please
by Arthur It is

Housework
by Dustin Cook

Mommy
Needs To Go To Detox

How to Survive in the Forest
by: Lawson D. Woods

Kidney Functions
by: I.P. Daley

Common Cold Symptoms
by Ron E. Nose

Carpet Fitting
by Walter Wall

Fix Your Car
Mick Annick

Swimming in the Ocean
by C. Lyons

Carnival Rides
by Ivana Herl

Dieting
by Les Tweet

Gone Fishing
by Rod Enreel

Growing up in the Balkans
by Hugo Slavia

Flips And Tumbles
by Jim Nastics

Green Spot on The Wall
by Picken & Flicken

Embarrassed in the Shower
by Kurt N. Fell

The Squeaky Gate
by Rusty Hinges

Turkish Minerals
by Asa Miner

Three Wishes
by Al Adin

Dog Snacks
by Nora Bone

The Constable's Job
by Lauren Awter

Constipation
by Anita Pu

Turkish Fast Food
by Donna K. Bab

Twist and Shout
by Sheikh Tall-About

Picnicking
by Alf Resco

The Lost Coffin
by Sue Anne Undertaker

Woulda Been a Great Shortstop
by Buddy Kent Hitt

You're Kidding!
by Shirley U. Jest

Pilgrim Settlers
by May Flower

Webster's Words
by Dick Shunnary

Gunslingers With Gas
by Wyatt Burp

The History of Exxon
by Phil Errup

Star Spangled Barrio
by José Canusee

Great Britain From 1837 to 1910
by Vic Torian and Ed Wardian

Maritime Disasters
by Andrea Doria

Military Defeats

by Major Disaster and General Mayhem

A Thousand Years Ago

by Ben A. Round

What's For Dinner?

by Chuck Roast

Blushing

by Rosie Cheeks

Beekeeping

by A. P. Arry

Cooking Spaghetti

by Al Dente

Two Thousand Pounds!

by Juan Tonn

All-You-Can-Eat Buffets

by I.M.A. Piggee

Achy Breaky Heart

by Anne Guish

Advanced Math

by Somar T. Pants

25 Ways to Prepare Hot Dogs

by Frank Fuhrter

The Art of Deception

by Miss Leed Ing

A Breath of Fresh Air

by Hal E. Tosis

A Poke in the Eye

by Dee Stick

Are You Dancing?

by R. U. Asking

Back Problems

by Eileen Bent

Harassment
by Percy Q. Shun

Intellectual Isolation
by Ivory Towers

I Love You!
by Rhea Lee with Alma Hart

After The Corned Beef and
Cabbage
by Kay O'Pectate

How to Cook a Steak
by Porter House

A Guide to Adhesives
by Stieg Ing

Hiya Fella
by Gladys Eeya

I Beat Bobby Fischer
by Jess Player

Lotsa Luck

by Bess Twishes

The Winter Olympics

by: Bob Sled

Volunteer's Guidebook

by Linda Hand

My Daily Ablutions

by Guindere Npoop

Make Your Pizza Italian

by Pepé Roney

Pasta Delicacies

by Liz Anya

Happy New Year!

by Mary Christmas

Nordic Groundskeepers

by Leif Raker

Italian Recipes

by Beau Napatito

Armed Robbery

by Andy Tover

Italian Cooking

by Mac Aroni

Arriba

by Juan Tan Amera

The Philippine Post Office

by Imelda Letter

You Can Be Both!

by Wong N. Wite

The Great English Breakfast

by Chris P. Bacon

Everything
I Want to Do
Is Illegal

SATIRE
HOME & GARDEN
BUSINESS
CHILDREN'S
HEALTH
MYSTERY
TRAVEL
SCIENCE

Mexican Revenge

by Monty Zuma

Irish Dentistry

by Perry O'Dontal

Irish First Aid

by R.U. O 'Kaye

Small Vegetables

by Russell Sprout

Organic Vegetables

by Hedda Lettuce

Greeting Sheep Strangers

by Hugh R. Ewe

The Smorgasbord

by Buffy Dinner

Tinseltown Tales

by Holly Wood

To Be Honest

by Frank Lee

The Excitement of Trees

by I. M. Board

Solving Crimes

by Dee Tectiff

Indiana Jones' Adventures

by Darrin Rescue

Money Management

by Owen Cash

Vegetable Arrangements

by Art E. Choke

Lawn Care

by Ray King

Lots of Excitement

by Hugh N. Cry

Life in the Sorority House
by Carrie Onn

The Greasy Pan
by Chris Coe

What Makes Airplanes Go
by Jeff Fuel

You Drip!
by Lee K. Fawcette

Roadside Signs
by Bill Board

Equally Adept
by Amber Dextrous

Men Can Change
by Betty Woant

The Hidden Surprise
by Pam Perz

A Hole in the Roof
by Lee King

You're a Bundle of Laughs
by Vera Funny

Mineralogy for Giants
by Chris Tall

Gunslingers with Gas
by Wyatt Urp

And the Other People
by Allan Sundry

You're So Sweet
by Mabel Syrup

I Win!
by U. Luz

The Proctologist's Handbook
by Ben Dover

Scuffed Floors

by Mark Tupp

Snorting My Way to Heaven

by Angel Dust

Season Tickets

by Oprah Maven

Singin' At the Met

by Oprah Tick-Tenor

And the Other People

by Allan Sundry

The Paper Route

by Avery Daye

The Auto Salvage Business

by: Rex Toad

Acrophobia

by Alfredo Heights

The Nude Beach

by Seymour & Howe

Why Did You Leave Me?

by Noe Clew

When the Outboard Motor Died

by I. Rhoda Shaw

Star Wars

by Rho Botts

Late For Work

by Dr. Wages

Jaws

by Tay Kabite

Party Game

by Bob Frapples

The Wizard Of Oz

by Ima Munchkin

The Hungry Baby
by Nora Titoff

Pakistani Covid Precautions
by Soshal Disdan Singh

Old Lang Syne Gunnar de Daze
Hurricane on the Horizon
by Gus deWinds

Something's Fishy
by Ann Chovie

Overweight Vegetables
by O. Beets

Tyrant of the Potatoes
by Dick Tater

Sex Hawaiian Style
by Kamanauana Leia

Chest Pain
by I. Coffalot

Learnabout....
SPITTING ON
CAKES

How to Get Rid of Unwanted
Guests
by Bea Rude

More for Your Money
by Max Amize

Smash Her Lobster!
by Buster Crabbe

Downsizing
by Lester Worribout

Make Your Own Honey
by B. Keeper

Ready for Bed
by P.J. Maws

Gut Wrenching Rides
by Rollie Coaster

The Billionaire's Son
by Rich Kidd

Promoting Your Product
by Brandon Close

Role Models
by Anne Spire-Ng

Statues
by Stan Dingstel

Weak Bladder
by I.P. Offen

Defunct Nations
by Sophie Etyunian

Going Nuclear
by Adam Baum

Children's Books That Didn't Make It

(and you should probably avoid)

You Are Different and That's Bad

The Boy Who Died from Eating All
His Vegetables

Fun four-letter Words to
Know and Share

Hammers, Screwdrivers and Scissors:
An I-Can-Do- It Book

The Kids' Guide to Hitchhiking

Kathy Was So Bad Her Mom Stopped
Loving Her

Curious George and the
High-Voltage Fence

All Cats Go to Hell

The Little Sissy Who Snitched

Some Kittens Can Fly.

That's it, I'm Putting You
Up for Adoption

Grandpa Gets a Casket

The Magic World Inside the
Abandoned Refrigerator

Garfield Gets Feline Leukemia

The Pop-Up Book of Human Anatomy

Strangers Have the Best Candy

Whining, Kicking and Crying to Get
Your Way

You Were an Accident

Things Rich Kids Have, But
You Never Will

Pop! Goes the Hamster...And Other
Great Microwave Games

The Man in the Moon Is
Actually Satan

Your Nightmares Are Real

Where Would You Like to Be Buried?

Eggs, Toilet Paper, and Your School

Why Can't Mr. Fork and Ms.
Electrical Outlet Be Friends?

Daddy Drinks Because You Cry

Also

by Andrew A. Felder

from the pages of **thenetwork**

The Best Diversions

Give yourself the gift of smiles. ☺

A handsome, artbook-style volume with the best Diversions to appear in **thenetwork** over the last decade. A compendium you will treasure for years to come.

"This collection is laugh-out-loud funny!"
Kirkland Review of Books

"Prescription: Read 3–4 pages a day for a month. It'll brighten your day! And make it last a month."
Susan Carnegie, The Montreal Voice

From Where I Sit

The Editor's Page in **thenetwork** is almost totally devoted to humor and wisdom and this is a collection of some of the best of them. Go to www.crestnetwork.com and **get the digital book for free!**

Vertical Lines

A Compilation of **Sarcasm, Word Play, and Witticisms** from the pages of **thenetwork**.

"This is simply genius. I kept on laughing the whole day when I read it."
Maria Tariq

"...absolutely hilarious! I laughed so hard that it brought tears to my eyes."
Randal Maynard

also from The CREST Publications Group

My Hand Book

"Incisive yet expansive - as if the psychology of R.D. Laing encountered the self-exploration of Hugh Prather to help readers delve into their own thought, experiences and behaviours."
The Rockford Tribune

"Curiously intense and ironic. This is a work that will make you think and feel and you will revisit it over and over."
Marion Danziger, The Toronto Town Crier

Leading With My Heart

"It matters not who we have been, or why, with whom, or how. What matters is that we have met and who we are from now."

Original reflections on new love, its flame, intensity, and all-consuming spirit. Short, poetic expressions of heartfelt longing, passion, and desire. Intimate expressions of tenderness and adoration, accompanied by romantic pictures. A wonderful gift for someone you love.

"So simple. So eloquent and beautiful. Absolutely wonderful!"
Allison Templeton

S.H.I.T. from the Internet

"An often off-color (but always entertaining and almost always hilarious) collection of jokes that you will read, enjoy – and probably tell – over and over."
Joey Cousins, The Greenwich Times

All available at
Amazon, BarnesAndNoble, Alibris
and in the Apple Book Store.

See a sample of each of the books at www.crestnetwork.com